HOW TO HAVE AN AFFAIR
AND NOT GET CAUGHT

by Lauren Tallman

The enclosed information is solely a guide based on many knowledgeable sources and personal opinions. There is no 100% guarantee for desired results

.

Dedicated to all those who seek an affair and who understand the importance of keeping it their deepest secret.

In Gratitude

I would like to thank all the trusting people who divulged their personal experiences toward the "True Story" sections.

Warm thanks to my family who stands by me, no matter what I write.

Most of all, my profound thanks to Leslie, who became my guiding angel.

INTRODUCTION

Do It Right

You decided to have an affair.

Moments are now filled with fantasies about meeting a mysterious stranger, rendezvous taking place in dark locations, stolen kisses and the promise of passion to come.

You may even have taken your first step and met someone. Maybe you've already managed a furtive tryst with a new partner.

Are you riding a wave of euphoria frantically planning your next date, or are you freaking out about getting discovered?

With this guide you will learn how to significantly and almost entirely reduce your chances of getting caught. Yes, here are helpful tips on how to have a "safe" affair, but it's going to take preparation and a little know-how.

Affairs can be dangerous, if not planned properly.

This book will help keep your home and family intact while making the most of the affair. Half the fun of an indiscretion is the spontaneity, but there's much at stake, especially if there are people you love whose feelings and lives may be at risk. For this reason, you will be making some extensive changes in your life to accommodate your plans.

To have a safe affair, you must think ahead. In short, you must be responsible or get out of bed!

The Long and the Short of It

There are two types of affairs – short term and long term.

One-night stands or a handful of convenient trysts are considered short term affairs. During a short-term affair, don't feel obligated to fill in your new companion about the details of your life, which include your full name, address, profession, family, etc. There is no reason for them to know so much personal information. Many tend to even lie at this stage simply due to safety precautions or to round out the fantasy. If you do make things up, keep it simple and easy to remember in case you decide to meet up again.

In a short-term affair never forget there are no strings attached and you owe each other nothing. No matter where or how you met, you both signed up for a short ride, not a lengthy adventure.

When short term affairs turn into long term affairs it usually means you've formed deep feelings for one another. When sincerity kicks in, it's time be honest. Be prepared to expose yourself to emotional involvement, but always be aware you are still having an affair, not a committed relationship. (See Chapter 7 "Where's This Thing Going?") In addition, emotions and affection will impair your judgment and this can lead to reckless decisions. Women fall prey to this recklessness much more easily than men. Women tend to think about how his last name sounds paired with hers, and even imagines her paramour leaving his life and, often, his wife for her. While women tend to commit faster, even men fantasize about a future together with their lover.

This is when you need to step into the cold shower of logic:

An affair is not a marriage proposal.
An affair is not a lifetime commitment.
An affair is an affair and nothing more.

At this point, if that cold shower gives you cold feet about having an affair, STOP NOW!!! If your conscience is bothering you while reading this, you're not ready. You still have time to go back.

But, if you're thinking, "Come on, get on with it. What do I need to do to have an affair responsibly?" then keep reading and remember, while you dream of that first kiss, and that first touch, you'll have to know how to handle the first-time perfume or aftershave lingers on your clothes, and the first time you'll have to settle up a motel bill.

That's what this book is all about!

Chapter 1

Ground Work

Time – Get It!

You need to make time for an affair.

Your family knows your routine. They know when you leave in the morning and when you come home at night. Without making a point of it, start changing your schedule slowly to build up your credibility.

Have coffee or grab a drink with a colleague or old friend after work without telling your family beforehand. Later, when asked where you were, tell the truth.

✓ Go window shopping for one hour on the way home, without mentioning it beforehand. Later, if asked, honestly say that you were looking at clothes or a new lawn mower.

✓ Choose the longest check-out lane in the supermarket. If you're asked why you're home later than usual, you can honestly say the supermarket was packed.

✓ Once in a while leave for work 20 minutes early. Mention that you want to beat the morning rush, to get to the office due to some extra work you have.

✓ You can easily give the same excuse on the flipside, by leaving work 20 minutes later. When coming home late, be honest and say you worked a little late at the office in order to beat heavy traffic out of the area.

✓ Never say you stayed at the office when you didn't because someone may have tried to call you there and your cover will be blown.

✓ Never lie and say you were late due to a traffic jam or an accident on the road if there wasn't one. Your spouse could have been listening to the radio or watching the news and will have heard that the roads were clear.

✓ Likewise, if you get paid for overtime, never use "staying late at the office" as an excuse for not coming home on time. The extra pay will not show up on your salary stub!

✓ If you can safely use "work" as an excuse, do not say you're working on a project with fellow employees. Your spouse may inadvertently ask one of them how the project is coming along.

Be honest in your answers! Don't lie because there is no need to lie. Get used to answering calmly and to the point. There is no reason to be nervous because you are not lying!

The more you make these little changes, the less self-conscious you will feel, and the more extra time you'll be adding to your daily away-from-home schedule (See Chapter 3 "Where Were You?")

If small children are involved, work your new schedule around them. This book will not advocate neglecting children for any reason.

Accessibility – Lose It!

Your family knows they can always get in touch with you at any time through your cell phone. Start changing that right away!

✓ Get out of the habit of answering the phone the moment it rings. Get caller ID on every phone you own, and if possible, on your work phone. When you see your better half is calling, don't pick up and don't call back for 10 minutes. Next time wait 20 minutes. But don't answer any other calls either. You can't take the chance that a family friend will say they spoke to you when you plan to tell your spouse you weren't near the phone.

✓ If asked why you didn't answer your phone, say the supermarket was so crowded and noisy and you just didn't hear it ring, or the traffic was so crazy you didn't want to risk taking your hands off the wheel. Whatever you say, make it believable. Take control of your phone. Don't jump when it rings.

Phones and Lovers

Since we're already talking about phones...

✓ NEVER speak to your lover on your home phone. NEVER give your spouse the chance to pick up the phone and hear your lover's voice asking to speak with you. NEVER give your spouse a reason to question a series of suspicious hang-ups. Speak with your lover about this and be insistent.

✓ If your lover should leave a suspicious voice message on any of your phones, others in your home or work may hear it! No messages should be left by either of you, on any phone.

✓ It is not wise to set up another mobile phone account, where you are billed at your office. Bills and statements could inadvertently find their way to your home. Just be very careful with the phone you have!

✓ If you speak to your lover on your cell phone always erase their number in the missed, received, or dialed lists. Only erase your lover's number. It will look suspicious if all your calls have been wiped out.

✓ Don't store your lover's number in your phone memory. Commit it to your memory instead. Have your lover do the same.

✓ Your phone call activity may be sent along with your phone statement. If your spouse needs those phone statements for business purposes, then DO NOT communicate with your lover on any phone that can be traced. If your spouse doesn't need to see a list, you can request from your phone company not to send you an itemized list every month.

✓ Plan ahead with your lover that when you hang up on them or say "Sorry, wrong number," they know that it means you were unable to speak freely. Make sure no one's feelings are hurt, and they know the rude hang-up is for the safety of everyone involved. Do not ever step out of the house or go into another room to talk on the telephone. It is insulting to everyone around you and a sure give away that you have a secret.

✓ Never whisper anything foolish like, "Can't talk now," or "I told you not to call me here." Don't whisper at all! And don't think coded language on the phone will help you out either. Coded sentences can only mean you have a secret.

True Story

While sitting with a couple, the husband received a phone call. He said it was "someone from the office" but we could still hear the stilted tête-à-tête. His wife, who happened to be sitting right next to me, whispered, "He's having an affair, isn't he?" This was of course a rhetorical question. It was embarrassing for everyone involved – and none of us should have been involved!

Make the Unusual Look Usual

Once your schedule is more your own, and you're not a slave to the phone, start shifting your activities.

If your work often entails late afternoon meetings, you will have a much easier time explaining why you come home late. Make sure your fictitious meetings "take place" outside the office.

Your marketing can also be your salvation.

✓ If you are the one buying the groceries, split up your shopping. Buy perishables when you have time but buy non-perishables on days when you're planning a tryst.

✓ Find a grocery that opens early which is near or on the way to work. On the days you're planning your rendezvous, have an exact list of what you need, leave the house early, and buy your non-perishables before you get to work. Even vegetables will keep in a cooler in the back of your trunk. Try placing the order the night before if you can. That way you can quickly pick up your groceries in the morning and be just a few minutes late for work.

✓ Buying your food in the morning can give you up to 2 hours of freedom later that day. Your excuse for coming home late that evening? 'The market was packed.' But make sure to say this only if you shop at a market far away from the prying eyes of your friends, neighbors, and spouse who could easily know if the local market was indeed crowded.

True Story

One acquaintance who had an affair did her shopping one summer morning but didn't have a cooler. She left two cantaloupes in the trunk of her car for the entire eight-hour workday. It took several service men in a local carwash, and a lot of air freshener to get the smell out. It also took hours of repeated explanations to her husband, who could not understand how melons could make the car smell so badly, thinking she had bought them only an hour before.

✓ Don't fool yourself by thinking you can pick up the groceries after your date, even if they're already bagged and waiting at the market. You'll never have the time.

✓ Never complain about the price of your produce at home. It may lead to a conversation about where and when you bought it!

✓ Always pay in cash. Credit card statements and receipts have times and dates printed on them, leaving a trail for others to follow, and find you out.

✓ On the days you're not planning to meet your lover, spend some quality time with the kids at the supermarket to get all the perishables you need, including ones they like, for the week ahead. Consider treating them to an ice cream cone too, but don't over compensate children if you're usually strict about these things. (See Chapter 9 "Keep Things Normal")

Camouflage Made Easy

Even if you make it home just 10 minutes before your spouse, it can still seem as if you've been home for hours.

✓ Learn how to make some quick and colorful meals that look complicated. For example, sprinkle almond slivers on plain boiled green beans, or dust some dried parsley on top of the mashed potatoes. Instead of spooning some rice on a dinner plate, press the rice into cookie cutters and place shaped rice patties on the plate. It will look like you took forever to prepare them. Your family will be so happy with your expert food preparation, they're bound to forget to ask where you've been and when you came back.

✓ Make the bed or just straighten the covers, crack out some new bars of soap in the bathroom, and rearrange some furniture. Quickly move or change items on the kitchen counter, on the living room coffee table, or the dining room table. Small changes like these make it seem like you've been at home for a while.

✓ Turn on the TV. If someone asks what you've been watching say you've been too busy to pay attention.

✓ If the children are home, do something distracting like playing loud music and dancing in their rooms while putting away their socks. They'll think you're nuts and forget when you really got home.

✓ Save these strategies for when you come home later than expected from your rendezvous. Don't use them unnecessarily.

True Story

A very resourceful friend came home far too late from a tryst to prepare a full dinner. Upon arriving home, she jumped into the shower and quickly washed her hair. She left the towel on her head as she prepared a "soup and sandwich" meal. Later, while the family ate, she apologized for the simple meal. She also mentioned that she'd had such a rough day and just had to take a long hot shower to straighten herself out. She gave the family extra dessert as compensation, which they didn't mind at all.

Chapter 2

Places to Meet

There Aren't Any

This isn't a joke. Unless your lover is single and lives alone you'll have nowhere to go! Fooling around in the back seat of a car can be fun and exciting in the beginning but after a while it feels sleazy and you will resent it.

Before you find a decent place to meet, you may only be able to share a few short moments together in some place off the beaten path. Do your best to stay away from areas that are unfamiliar to you, yet be on the lookout for safe, deserted fields or sites that could fit the bill. But check them out before going there at night.

✓ Never bring your lover to your home for any reason, unless you are unattached.

✓ Never go to your lover's home unless they are completely free from all ties. If their 'other half' catches you together, chances are the irate mate will call your other half out of spite.

Wherever your rendezvous takes place, do your best to drive in two separate cars. If seen, you'll never be able to explain why you were in a strange person's car.

True Story

A dear friend did not think far enough ahead when he asked the carwash attendant to "clean the car thoroughly". They removed all telltale signs of the tryst he'd had the

night before, except one. While driving the kids to a soccer game, one of his children looked up and said, "Daddy, what's that?" He adjusted his mirror as he drove, and suddenly saw a shoe print on the ceiling! He changed the subject, making them forget the odd question but during soccer practice he quickly scrubbed the car ceiling clean.

Using two cars also gives both of you the means to leave quickly, if one of you suddenly has to go home.

If either of you forgets something in the other's car, such as keys or underwear, forget about it! You'll get caught. Remember that strands of your lover's hair can be found on the headrest. You would be surprised at the odd things that can be left behind, things that you may not even notice, but your partner may.

True Story

A friend and her lover found a supposedly empty field and drove there in the dark. They made frantic love outside in the open. When it was over she turned her head and found a horse staring at her in the face. She almost had a stroke from the shock. Examine your chosen out-of-the-way spots in the light of day before planning your rendezvous.

In short, take two cars and find a reputable day-use as quickly as possible.

✓ Your best bet is to find a place that offers hourly or what's called "day-use" accommodations. These are sometimes called "no-tell motels" and are easily found on the net. Hotels are prominent and have neon advertisements outside. A day-use is usually an enclosed compound of cabins or rooms that is, as a rule, inconspicuous and charges on an hourly basis. Obviously, they offer the privacy that most hotels and motels can't offer. Call beforehand to check out rates and ask openly about their privacy policies.

✓ Many day-use places have cameras that survey the outside walks and parking areas. This isn't a bad thing! Before leaving the room, call the front desk and they will tell you to wait if someone is coming out of another room or if someone is in the parking area. This gives you another shot at absolute privacy.

✓ Find a place where you don't even have to go to a front desk area to "check-in" or "check-out." They may tell you to leave your money in a box outside the door of the cabin, as the manager will pick up the money after you have gone inside. There will be no need to ask for a key as it is already in the door, for you to lock from the inside. Again, total privacy.

✓ Never, ever, use your real names when reserving a room.

✓ Reputable day-use places will only accept cash. Credit card and check transactions only lead to enraged spouses storming their offices holding bank statements in their hand. You can only use cold cash. (See Chapter 6, "Money Matters")

✓ There should be individual and concealed parking spots just next to your cabin or room. If this isn't possible, choose a day-use where there's safe, off the main-street parking. Never let your car be seen in front of a hotel, motel, or day-use: even ones that are off the beaten track. Wherever you park, make sure it's legal. If you get a ticket, the time, date and street address will be printed on it! Spring for a garage and then throw away the receipt once you leave.

✓ Plan your meetings close to where you work. The small amount of extra mileage on the odometer will not cause any alarm. If you don't work, find a hide-a-way in the vicinity of the shopping malls or centers where you like to shop. But keep it as far from home as you can. It's that simple, yet very important.

✓ Once you find a hideaway, get a street map of the region.

✓ Find different routes that will bring you home from the day-use, from various directions and time them. Test the routes for speed traps, traffic jams and long lights. Don't take a road you haven't tested yet and don't make any markings of any kind on the map! Remove all cookies on your computer and phone regarding any routes!

✓ Watch the odometer. If you're adding too much mileage, then either change your meeting location or find another way home. Remember your map and keep to the shortest but safest routes.

True Story

A friend actually got her car stuck in a sand trap, trying to use an unexplored shortcut when coming home from a secret afternoon of passion. Luckily some truckers came along and hauled the car out. If they hadn't come along, it

would have taken the AAA forever to get there. Sheer luck kept my friend from getting found out.

Where You Said You Were

✓ Make a mental list of all the shops, museums, and book stores in the vicinity of your chosen rendezvous spot. In case someone sees you in the area you can easily explain why you were there.

✓ Casually mention to your spouse your renewed search for a perfect piece of clothing. Whether it's a perfect little black dress or the perfect holiday tie, these unattainables can be used as smoke screens to excuse your extra time away from home. When you're late coming home after some hours of passion and your spouse asks where you were, you can honestly say, "Oh, don't you remember, I told you I was looking for (fill in the blank). I have been looking for so long, and I almost bought an expensive one, but I decided to keep looking instead..." Once you start talking about it, your partner will lose interest and wish you were still out somewhere shopping.

✓ If you actually find that dress or tie you can then announce you need shoes, a bag, a scarf, jewelry, watch or jacket to go with it.

✓ This ruse also works well with household needs, such as faucets, looking for sinks later on, or carpets, and looking for matching lamps. The list is endless.

✓ Once in a while, buy some things for yourself or for the house, only to prove that you were shopping!

✓ Let's say you use a museum tour as a ruse to cover up a few hours with your lover. You must actually go there on the day you said you would! Take a few minutes to run through the place as this will give you material to talk about, should you be asked about it, and you will sound very convincing! If you see someone you know in the museum, all the better! Say "Hi" and smile and walk away. They'll never know you got out of there five minutes later. Back at home, if asked where you were, what could be more convincing than telling your spouse you had seen someone you know! You'll be in the clear. And again, once you babble on and on about the fabulous art and the lighting, etc., your spouse will probably not ask about your outings again.

✓ Get interested in new hobbies like sugar sculpting, bird watching, or geology hunts for long lost rock formations things that your family would never want to know about and certainly don't want to hear about. You might have to sugar sculpt a rose or two, but you can slip out of lectures and field trips easily enough and head out to a planned heavenly excursion of your own.

✓ A membership to a gym gives you the perfect excuse for coming home sweaty. This can be tricky, but if used properly, it's a shoo-in. Pick a gym that's not near your home but in the direction of where you hide away with your lover. Tell your spouse you will go three times a week. Plan on going to the gym twice a week. Go meet your lover on the third time. It's a great ploy because you'll actually get some exercise and after your secret meeting, you'll be able to come home sweaty and disheveled and go right into a shower – no questions asked!

True Story

My friend started going to the gym several times a week out of necessity. He usually ate dinner with his lover – whether it was an actual meal in her apartment or the cookies and coffee that came with the day-use room. When he came home in the evening, his family of course expected him to eat dinner with them too. The pounds began to show! While he used the gym as an excuse to get out of the house, he also used it to lose the extra weight.

Despite all your careful dodging, some spouses are just naturally overly suspicious. They may even hire a detective to make sure you're going to the places you say you go to. That's why all during your affair you must always be on high alert to notice if anyone is following you.

When you window shop, can you see anyone in the window reflection who stops walking whenever you do? When driving, is someone persistently taking all the turns you are? Hopefully it will never come to this.

Switch the days and times of your meetings. Use a number of day-use places, rather than frequenting only one. Just remember to keep your eyes open at all times.

Till now you were clever and never caught – but remember, you were also lucky. Be one step ahead and keep your guard up at all times.

True Story

The barrage of investigation shows on television gave a friend a very clever idea. She advised her lover to never buy

condoms or sex toys near their secret meeting place. There was a large mall just nearby, which was their individual excuses for being in that area. She realized that, should someone check up on them, any detective would find out that each had bought clothes or house wares, but never something intimate.

Chapter 3

"Where Were You?"

Staying Calm

You met with your lover and had a wonderful time. You're still on Cloud 9 when you walk through your door. Then you hear, "Where were you?"

There's no reason to panic, choke up, or lose your buzz. Keep in mind most people ask questions just to talk, not to really get information. Simply say whatever you had planned to say that day, whether it's the shopping excuse, or the gym answer, or the traffic retort. Then immediately ask if your spouse wants a snack. By the time you start serving something scrumptious, they will have forgotten about where you were, or that they even asked.

On the other hand, when your spouse is itching for an answer, that's when you start to talk, and talk and talk. Let's say you had used a car show as an excuse. Start talking about the things you actually saw there, the newest models, saying how fabulous it was, how the lighting made some chrome stand out more, that the antique cars on display were ones you had never seen before, and stress how your spouse would have just died if they had seen those odd-balls who came to see the exhibition.

Within five minutes, your partner would have had enough and maybe even asked you to stop talking about it. That's when you become understanding and tell them that of course they don't have to hear all about it. Then kiss them and make them some coffee and give them some cake. Make them feel as if they'd gotten off easy!

> ✓ What if you were seen? So, what! Stay calm or you'll lose control of the situation. If you hear, "Hey honey, Hank called and said he saw you down town," you stay calm and smile and say something noncommittal like, "That's nice." Since you

know you have a logical excuse tucked away for being downtown, don't continue. Leave it alone.

✓ On the other hand, if your spouse wants to hear about your outing, say you were shopping and then calmly talk about something else – the faucet that has been leaking, the walls that need painting, the laundry that needs to be washed or the rooms that need to be cleaned up. Your spouse will have forgotten all about Hank and run off because they don't want to hear about chores they should be doing.

✓ Oddly enough, people forget what they wanted to say when you talk about food. If you're having dinner and the kids ask where you were, answer simply and then ask if someone wants dessert. It works.

✓ Scenarios of how you will answer questions will come to mind, like little movie clips in your head. It will happen all the time, as you shower, when you drive, as you watch TV. Yes, it's normal and it's good! That means you're on your toes. You'll have gone through so many scenarios in your mind that it will be difficult to catch you off guard later. It will make you confident and feel prepared. Always remember how easy it is to change a subject, or get around a question, and also when to shut up.

✓ If you're a terrible liar then stand in front of a mirror when NO one is home and practice. Examine your expressions. Watch how you move. Is your body language saying something else? Practicing will make you feel better. Just make sure no one hears you!

✓ If an acquaintance or even a close friend ever confronts you or implies that you're having an affair, just laugh it off and change the subject. Ignore it. If you don't make an issue out of it, it means there is no truth to it. Don't try to deny it because it won't help, and you just may put emphasis on the question! Be calm and forget they asked.

True Story

Sitting with a colleague and a number of other employees, having a leisurely lunch outside the office, the conversation turned to more personal matters. When one employee blatantly asked my colleague if she was having an affair, my colleague (who, for a short moment, thought she would have a heart attack), quickly smiled, laughed the question off, and began speaking about "women's problems". This immediately had every woman around the table speaking about their personal experiences and ailments and took the focal point off of my colleague.

KISS – 'Keep It Simple Stupid'

✓ This is important. Don't get confused with too many details or explanations. Just keep things simple with excuses like "I'm off to the gym" and don't add extra information you'll never remember later.

✓ Don't be the first to speak when you get home. Always take into consideration you may have been seen. It would be totally awkward if you walked into the house talking about your workout at the gym when your husband has just been told that you were seen walking down a street in another neighborhood. Never walk into a lie voluntarily.

✓ Of course, you'll NEVER go to a movie theater with your lover, but you may see a movie in their house. Watch the movie and then forget you ever saw it. You may inadvertently mention a certain scene and your spouse will say, "Honey, we never saw that movie."

✓ Never go into detail about anything that has to do with your lover's interests. You may slip up, so it's better to just shut up.

True Story

Several years ago, the stores in our city were opened only half a day on Tuesdays. When my friend mentioned, in front of her husband and mine, that she'd bought her new skirt on Tuesday afternoon, I took her into another room and pointed out her slip-up. She said Tuesday afternoon was the only time she could get out to meet her lover. I explained that there was no need to specify when she'd

supposedly bought the skirt...and next time, to use her head before speaking!

True Story

A colleague told me how he came home after an evening with his lover. Unfortunately, the evening had run later than usual, and he didn't have time to shower at the day-use. While getting undressed in their bedroom, he was speaking to his wife when he had the urge to scratch his behind. There he found the ripped off section of a condom wrapper stuck to one cheek! Luckily, he crumbled it in his hand and got rid of it before his wife could see.

Chapter 4

Two People Can Keep A Secret If One of Them Is Dead

No, You Cannot Tell!

Never tell anyone about your affair. The moment someone else finds out about it, you'll be in danger of losing it all.

It's only normal to want to share the excitement, sing your lover's praises and gloat about their sexual prowess but you can't. Instead, talk to yourself when you drive. Write their name on the water when you bathe. You can smile that secret sated smile when you're with friends, but you can only own up by saying you're happy with your life, your work, or your dog learned a new trick.

As much as you want to speak about it, never insinuate you have a lover. Sorry, but those are the rules. Telling your best friend can put them in a terrible position – so don't do it.

Your friend may start treating you and your spouse differently and may even tell their significant other and that person may blab. And never use a friend as a cover, saying you were with them. It always backfires.

True Story

A friend used me as an excuse one evening. I'll never forget when her husband called our house to ask to speak to his wife. When I suddenly realized that she had used me as a 'wing-man', without telling me beforehand, it took a lot of double talk to get out of it. I tried to call her after I spoke to her husband, but she wouldn't answer her cell phone during her rendezvous. The couple since divorced.

Now let's talk about your lover. You must be sure that your companion will not tell their very best friend about you either. Speak openly about your expectations and agree that no one else is to know. If you find your lover is more interested in bragging than keeping a secret, drop your lover fast – no matter how good they are in bed!

Love at Work

Try not to have an affair with someone at work. It's hard enough to keep an affair undetected at home, but at work, it's nearly impossible. It will be difficult not to smile to your lover during working hours, or call them, or use the inter-office email to send a love note. Most computer programs save sent messages on the company's network server. Learn how to quickly delete messages and erase your email history. (See further in this chapter "Internet Savvy")

If you have an office affair, it will make it very difficult for your spouse to come visit and call. Many spouses like to meet for lunch or dinner or call during the day. A sudden unwillingness to meet or speak will look fishy.

If your spouse shows up at your job unexpectedly, make it short and sweet and get them out of the office quickly, without raising suspicion. Your spouse could easily pick up on a vibe by noticing something as simple as an exchanged smile between you and your co-worker/lover. Your lover may even confront your spouse with a look of triumph, possession or guilt.

True Story

A manager in a company had taken a day off 'for personal reasons' and asked to only be contacted on his cell phone, and only in case of emergency. Actually, he had taken his lover, a colleague of his at work, for a trip. Later, when his wife was planning a vacation, his salary report showed that he was missing a vacation day, which he couldn't explain.

Got the picture? An office affair is very risky and yet many affairs happen there. Why? Perhaps it's the adventure, or the convenience of not having to find someone who is far away. Whatever the reason, separate your love life from your work life. If that's not possible, then you and your lover will have to learn not to touch one another "by chance" as you pass in the halls. Someone will see it! Learn not to look in each other's direction. Treat them like a desk – something you sit near but have no interest in. Doesn't sound easy? It's not!

Internet Savvy

There must be someone you know who is pretty knowledgeable about computers. Start by asking them how to delete files. Have them explain how to delete your email history and delete your cookies (especially if you were surfing the net for sex toys or day-use locations).

If this is all Greek to you, then take this crash course on Computer Safety 101.

✓ If you must use the computer to communicate with your lover, set up a new email address through a server that doesn't charge a fee. Delete all incoming emails from your lover. Then delete all the deleted items in your Trash before closing your computer.

✓ You're asking for trouble if you have long text conversations on the computer late at night. Your spouse may sleep like a rock when you watch TV next to them, or when you read a book with the light on, but if you spend long nights on the computer, your spouse will get curious and want to find out what you're doing.

✓ Don't suddenly turn off the computer the moment someone in your family walks into the room, or if a colleague walks into your office. Learn how to minimize the screen quickly when emailing or reading email from your lover.

✓ Be sure your screen is turned away from others so no one else can see what you're writing! Make sure no one can stand behind you without you realizing they are there.

✓ Keep any nightly internet visits short and remember, delete, delete, delete.

True Story

A fellow employee kept a mirror on her desk, situated so that it allowed her to see if someone was coming up behind her. The moment she saw movement in the mirror, she had enough time to minimize her screen and no one saw the love notes she was sending to her lover.

Pick Up Your Toys

Your lover may introduce you, or you may introduce your lover, to sex toys. Do your best not to take these toys home with you, especially if you have small children in the house. They find everything!

If you must bring them home, it's imperative you locate a spot where you're sure no one can ever find them. No, the top shelf of your closet is not a good idea. Kids climb up on chairs. The garage isn't a good place either. You know your house. Find the safest place!

Pillow Talk

Has your spouse ever told your friends how you talk in your sleep and actually thought it was funny? That means you may never call your lover by their name, because it may slip out when you're sleeping! Even in moments of passion, call your lover some universal endearment like "Darling" or "Dear."

Speak to your lover and ask if they talk in their sleep. Many people do. If they turn pale when you ask, you'll know they have to take the same precautions.

Chapter 5

Perfumes, Makeup and New Clothes

Getting Ready

Start using a body cream, aftershave, perfume or cologne that's a little stronger than the one you usually use. A good body cream will keep you safe from any odors, natural as they are.

✓ If you don't want to put creams in sensitive areas, try some hair conditioner or baby oil after your shower. They have pleasant fragrances and will be less likely to cause an irritation.

✓ Get those plastic travel bottles that are small but seal well. Fill them with lubricant or cream. One can hold toothpaste or mouth wash. Keep a pack of wet ones in the car or carry a small pack in your bag. Your best bet is to have a small bag with all these items at work. This way you can freshen up before a rendezvous if it's after work hours. There are showers or Jacuzzis in the day-use place but at least you'll come in smelling like a rose.

✓ Always carry some of your chosen fragrance with you too. Just in case you can't squeeze in a shower before you go home, you can splash or spray some on before you return to your spouse.

✓ Never give your spouse a perfume or cologne your lover uses. Forget it. Never! Your spouse could smell it on you and wonder how it got on your clothes when you hadn't see them all day.

✓ Don't remove a child's seat or childrens' toys from the car on the assumption that it makes you look attached (which you are) or single (which you're not). It will look suspicious to the family when they find the seat out of place or the toys stored in the trunk, so just try not to break them during a quickie in the back seat.

✓ Don't take your wedding ring off before your rendezvous. Make believe it's not there. One day you'll forget to put it back on and that will only hurt your spouse and possibly your children when they see you're not wearing it. Your lover doesn't care if you have a ring on your finger or in your nose. Just leave it on and forget it.

Looking Good

✓ Women will wear full makeup more often now and should start wearing makeup every day, even when at home. If someone notices and asks why you're wearing it, smile and ask if it looks good. Laugh and feel pretty. Let your makeup become part of your everyday life, without making a fuss about it, and no one will notice it later on. This way when you get all dolled up to meet your lover, you won't look different than on the days when you're not planning a date. Plus, good makeup can cover any unwanted love bites you may get during passionate lovemaking. Of course, you will make sure that your lover does not leave any marks, and you will speak to them about it. (See Chapter 8 "Am I Getting Through to You Yet?")

✓ Men will shave closer and wear a finer aftershave and should do this every day. If asked why, say you've gotten into the habit because work necessitates you looking well-groomed.

✓ Start dressing a little better every day, making it less conspicuous when you get dolled up for your rendezvous. Don't go overboard or make drastic changes to your wardrobe right away. Instead, buy new things gradually or buy accessories that will update and embellish the clothing you already have. If someone mentions you're dressing "better than ever these days", just smile and say, "Thank you." It was a compliment. No explanations needed.

✓ Wear clothing to your rendezvous that doesn't wrinkle. Yes, synthetic clothing may feel uncomfortable – hot in the summer and cold in the winter – but you cannot imagine how many times your clothes will be thrown aside in the heat of passion. You can say the seat belt in the car crushed the front of your shirt, but that answer won't fly if your pants legs are crumpled too! Don't worry. You'll only wear these clothes for a rendezvous, so just buy something that looks good on you.

✓ You may want to buy sexy new underwear too, but that will get noticed at home super quick. Wear it without making a fuss. Don't hide it either. The new underwear may turn on your spouse, but if you really don't want to be with them sexually, just get dressed and undressed in another room. If someone at home asks about your new undergarments, just say, "It was on sale."

✓ If you start a diet at the same time you update your wardrobe and your makeup or hairstyle, you might as well put a neon sign on your forehead that says, "I'm having an affair!" If you're having a short-term affair, there's no need to take drastic steps to alter your looks. If you're involved in a long-term affair, you'll have the time to make all the changes you want gradually.

✓ Should your lover give you a gift, whether it's jewelry, a new perfume, a wallet, or anything, you have a problem. If your spouse sees it and asks about the new item, don't panic. Treat the item with little importance. If asked how much it cost, have a reasonable sum in mind.

✓ When using sex toys, buy an inconspicuous bag or briefcase with several compartments. Fill, empty, or hide it when no one is home. The last thing you want is your spouse or child to barge into a room to find you with a gold vibrator in your hand. Never leave this bag lying around either, in case someone wants a piece of gum and decides to look inside!

Chapter 6
Money Matters

It Matters If It's Not on Hand

Having an affair costs money. If you don't have one already, it's time to open your own bank account. This makes it easier to have cash on hand and to adjust your own accounts.

✓ Men may want to pay most of the expenses of an affair, out of sheer excitement. Women may want to go Dutch out of common courtesy or self-esteem. Either way, go with the flow, but make sure no one feels used.

✓ Additional money is also important because when having an affair, you'll need to buy some extras (See Chapter 5 "Perfumes, Makeup and New Clothes"), for inflated telephone bills, extra gas for the car, parking fees, day-use charges, or fare for a cab.

If your spouse handles the accounting at home there are ways of saving money here and there that will not seem conspicuous.

✓ Using cash will give you liquid assets that will go right into your pocket. If your spouse doesn't check the bills, keep the change from any purchase. You'll be surprised how quickly this adds up!

✓ Cut back on household expenses and reduce the grocery bill. Buy chopped frozen vegetables rather than whole fresh ones. Buy fruits that are in season and don't buy priccy exotic ones. Bring home daisies rather than roses. No one will notice these changes, but it will mean more money in your pocket.

✓ Instead of buying expensive cosmetics and toiletries, buy ones on sale or lower priced ones at bargain stores. Consider making your own too. You can find recipes for facial scrubs on the internet.

✓ Start bringing unassuming and healthy lunches to work rather than eating out all the time. If someone at home asks why you're taking a bag with you, say it's for a late afternoon snack. This is so logical that no one will ask you again. But keep the money you would have spent on those overpriced lunches at the Deli. You'll be eating healthier and will probably lose weight!

✓ Pay attention to all kinds of sales advertised in the papers. When you buy something on sale, don't mention the lowered price and keep the difference in your pocket. Throw away all receipts.

✓ Instead of buying an expensive gift for a friend, make a homemade present, or bake something. A cake you make yourself is a tenth of the price of a store bought one and people really appreciate the trouble you went through.

✓ Don't buy unnecessary items at the grocery. Use whatever canned goods you have in the house before buying extras. If you usually buy two packs of cigarettes, gum, or candy, buy one instead and keep the extra money in your pocket.

✓ NEVER take large amounts out of a joint account at one time! If you have your own account, be sure no one sees your bank or credit card statements.

✓ Saving money is a big burden on anyone having an affair because spouses may not pay attention to many things, but they always watch the money. So, watch yourself!

HOW TO HAVE AN AFFAIR AND NOT GET CAUGHT   43

✓ Saving money is a big burden on anyone having an affair because spouses may not pay attention to many things, but they always watch the money. So, watch yourself!

True Story

A recently divorced friend had done the unimaginable – he had actually used his credit card to buy his girlfriend a gift. Of course, when his wife looked at the bank statement, she knew that she had never received jewelry from the very expensive shop. He learned the hard way that if he didn't have a large amount of cash on hand, he should have waited until he saved it up, or put a down payment on the jewelry and paid it off, in cash.

Chapter 7

Where's This Thing Going?

Questions for You, Questions About Your Lover

What do you expect from this affair?

- ✓ Friendship? That's possible.
- ✓ Sex. For sure!
- ✓ Love? Not likely.
- ✓ A life together? That's an unrealistic dream.

How does your lover handle this affair?

- ✓ Are they responsible at keeping secrets and having safe sex?

- ✓ Are they considerate and kind to you or do they only care about sex?

- ✓ Do they understand this could never go farther than an affair and anything more would only put you both in harm's way?

Separate love from lust. They are two different emotions. Love is a strong affection with personal ties. Lust is an intense longing based solely on desire. Be honest with yourself, and with your lover. Which do you really feel?

Eventually you'll both have to decide whether you want to keep this affair short or stay the course. Ask questions. It's your right to know where the other stands. There's a fine line between having an affair and having a relationship and you shouldn't mix up the two.

✓ Whatever your lover tells you, take it with a grain of salt. Your lover will be looking out for their own interests and concentrate on prolonging good bedroom activity. They may not care for you as a partner in life, just a partner in the sack. They'll often answer questions by telling you what you want to hear. Be alert!

✓ If you find your lover isn't looking out for you or your feelings, think twice about continuing the affair. Is it worth the fear, the anxiety, and the possible loss of your family?

✓ Make sure you're satisfied in bed. If your lover just wants a quickie and gets up and runs to the door after a few minutes of fun, dump them now. Going through so much trouble for so little is not only insulting, it also puts you in unnecessary jeopardy. If all you want is the quick sex, then this does not pertain to you.

True Story

My friend was having a wonderful time meeting her lover only once a week, though holidays and family commitments sometimes kept them apart two weeks at a time. When they suddenly had the opportunity to meet more often, she felt they were growing closer emotionally. Instead of an affair that was non-committal and plain fun, it was turning into a relationship, which neither of them wanted. They talked it over, realizing that it was actually endangering their happy and unobtrusive affair. They wholeheartedly agreed to go back to their once-a-week arrangement.

✓ When one of you is married, know from the beginning that the affair will never turn into a serious relationship. It's a sexual affair, possibly an intense one, but not a never-ending relationship. Make sure you both make the distinction. Never base your affair on false expectations. Ideally it should revolve around fun and mutual respect.

✓ Don't make promises you cannot keep. Nothing will make your lover reveal your affair to your spouse quicker than your failure to fulfill an insincere commitment to end your marriage for them.

During a long-term affair meeting will become more and more frequent and crucial to your need to be with one another. It means taking more time away from your home and family, which may eventually lead to divorce.

If your affair turns into a legitimate relationship, the two of you have to seriously talk about the future and figure out if you both are willing to split up your families. At this point, there is a lot at stake and you both must think long and hard about it.

You and your lover must go to a lawyer together and get advice. It's imperative your lover comes with you. If they aren't willing to go now, they won't ever make a real commitment to you any time later on. You need to make sure your lover is, at all times, just as serious as you are about where your relationship is going, if you plan on ending your marriage.

First and foremost, look out for #1. You must make sure that you are safe and that you won't lose everything in the end.

True Story

A close friend was broken-hearted when her lover, who had made a load of promises, backed out at the very last minute. "Always get a diamond, a big one, or a signed agreement made out by a lawyer!" she said. "You need solid proof that he is really sincere!" She was very lucky that she did not end her marriage before she had conclusive proof that her lover was willing to end his.

Chapter 8

You Never Did That Before!

Safety First

Picking out a piece of toast from the toaster with a fork may kill you.

Having sex without a condom *will* kill you.

As you plan your affair with your soon-to-be lover, the first thing to talk about is having safe sex. If you're too embarrassed to bring up the subject of safe sex, condoms and AIDS tests, then you're not ready to have an affair. When you have an affair, you need to be in control of your health, your body, and your expectations.

You both can get tested for AIDS quickly and anonymously. Until you see your new prospective lover's clean bill of health, no bodily liquids may be exchanged.

If your lover doesn't insist that you take the AIDS test, it means they didn't make their last lover take one either, or the one before that, or the one before that. Step away now!

Keep in mind that, without a condom, you are having sex with everyone your lover has ever been with.

✓ There's no reason in the world to have unprotected sex. Don't fall for the lines about condoms restricting motion or sensation. In addition to AIDS leading to a horrific death, hepatitis kills more people than AIDS. Even if you take AIDS tests, you can never know what other diseases may be lurking around in your lover's system.

✓ Genital herpes and syphilis can be passed along to your spouse. You must be protected at all times!

✓ Don't consider oral sex without condoms either. There should be no playing with genitals without a condom. Remember, pre-ejaculation secretion is just as dangerous as ejaculation discharge. If necessary, look through the vast amount of reputed medical sites on the net to give you reliable advice and suggestions regarding safe sex.

✓ Don't use birth control pills or menopause as excuses to not use condoms. Pregnancy isn't the main point. You still need condoms. They are the only thing that could stand between you and disaster.

True Story

A close acquaintance sat pale and shaken when he told me about a lovely woman he had recently been seeing. When things became 'hot and heavy', he asked that she take an AIDS test. Gentleman and responsible person that he is, he also took the test and immediately brought her the results. Twice, she gave excuses about forgetting hers or she had left it in another bag. "I half expected her to say her dog ate it," he said sadly. When she didn't show up with her results the third time, he stopped the almost-affair, wondering what she had to hide!

Am I Getting Through to You Yet?

Read all about safe sex, until you're scared enough to always use a condom.

✓ Never take condoms from the house if that's what you also use at home. Your spouse will notice that some are missing.

✓ Never bring home extras, left over from your tryst, because the expiration dates or lot numbers will be different than what you have at home. Most people don't look at expiration dates on cereal boxes or soda cans, but they look at expiration dates on condom boxes!

✓ Never bring condoms into the house especially if your husband has had a vasectomy or if your wife is on the pill.

✓ You or your lover will have to bring the condoms each time you meet. If your lover refuses to bring them, or says they forgot them, walk out. Leave. If your lover isn't responsible enough to care about your health and life or theirs, you should not be with them.

✓ In the beginning, everyone should be prepared to get minor yeast or bladder infections and even canker sores. While it's best to get treatment from your doctor, don't get overly excited about these afflictions. Being in contact with someone else's perfume or cologne, aftershave or body creams, hotel sheets and blankets, to say nothing of your lover's saliva, can breed these problems. Give your body time to adjust to the new elements.

✓ If your lover arrives with a camera, take out the batteries and put it all away. Make sure there are no pictures of you in compromising positions – ever! If someone gets a hold of your picture, it will cause embarrassment, can lead to blackmail, and will certainly be grounds for divorce.

Just to make sure you remember, I repeat, you must *always* make sure that no bodily fluids pass between you until you see all the medical tests indicating a clean bill of health from both of you.

Now let's get on to the lighter side of this affair.

Love making with your spouse has probably become less passionate throughout the years. You get into regular habits during love making and oddly enough, it's not that common for a long standing married couple to get sex toys or try new positions.

On the other hand, a lover is a surefire aphrodisiac, with whom you get to play with your bodies differently than what you're used to. You'll probably be much more open and curious about new positions, toys and games. You will try techniques and positions you would never dare suggest to your spouse.

✓ Don't go home and tell your spouse you'd like to make love while hanging from the chandelier (like you did the day before with your lover). Your spouse will wonder where these ideas came from!

✓ You should speak seriously with your lover if there are some techniques or positions you would never use. An affair is for fun, not control.

✓ If your lover likes to scratch, tell them to stop. No hickeys, either. Neither of you should go home to your partners with telltale evidence on your bodies. If your lover doesn't agree, get up and leave.

✓ If you drink any alcohol during your rendezvous make sure it's at the very beginning to ensure you'll be sober for the ride home. If you are stopped for drunk driving, you're as good as caught red handed. Drink water or coffee before you leave to dilute the alcohol level in your bloodstream. Also chew on a serious breath mint before and during your car ride home.

Chapter 9

Keep Things Normal

What Comes First

You may feel guilty about your passionate hours away from home and have a compulsion to "make up for lost time" with the family. Take it easy. There's no need to overcompensate. Take this quick test. If you don't answer YES to all of the following, you need to think again about having an affair and reprioritize your focus and activities.

✓ Do you always make sure that the family comes first?

✓ Do you and your lover accept the fact that either of you may have to go home sooner, or may suddenly call off a rendezvous altogether, because you are needed at home?

✓ You try not to overcompensate the kids with extra toys or paint their bedroom to show you care.

✓ You didn't forget old habits like putting your arm around your spouse when you fall asleep.

✓ You found you may have become a little indifferent to your family and you stopped the affair for a while and got yourself back on track with them.

Never make your affair the #1 priority in your life.
That spot is reserved for your family.
Your lover is reserved for fun.

And try not to lose touch with your usual group of friends even if you feel a tendency to withdraw from them. They'll be the first ones to question you about where you've been hiding yourself.

Sometimes you will find yourself distracted and daydreaming about your secret life. It will look odd to your family when you're sitting at the dinner table, staring into space and smiling widely, while eating Brussel sprouts.

Get back into focus.

Tired? You Bet!

You'll sleep longer and harder than before because having an affair is mentally and physically exhausting as well as time consuming. Unconscious tension will sap your strength. Try taking short naps whenever you can to keep up your energy at home and at work.

True Story

I was sitting in a restaurant with my friend (who was having a raging affair) while her husband and mine were engrossed in a conversation about sports. When I looked up from my salad, I saw she had actually fallen asleep, chin in hand, which was bad enough but her beautiful long curls were dipping into her salad dressing. I gave her a short kick under the table. She quickly excused herself, running to clean off her shirt where her hair had left oily streaks.

✓ If your spouse complains about you falling asleep early each night, or that you don't pay attention to them anymore, send the kids to your parents on Saturday mornings. Spend that quality time with your spouse in bed and catch up on your sleep afterwards.

✓ Set aside a few moments every day to relax with your spouse, to talk about the kids, the house, the car.

✓ Play games with the kids, watch TV with them, make them hot chocolate and just sit and talk.

✓ Take some time to meet up with old friends just to enjoy a cup of coffee.

✓ Find some time to relax alone. Listen to soft music, catch up on your reading, or take a short nap or meditate.

✓ Never let yourself get overtired or cranky. This is when mistakes are made. Take care of yourself.

Tiger in A Cage

Don't fall victim to the "Tiger in A Cage" syndrome. That's when you pace around the house wishing you were really having sex with your lover. It's when you look out the window, in the direction of your rendezvous spot, grasping the sill with your hands while your heart is beating a mile a minute. Do your best to control these episodes. It will happen because you are sexually aroused, and your adrenaline is pumping.

When all you can think about is grabbing your keys and running out of your house to meet your lover somewhere, you must calm down. Remember that your lover is with their family too and probably can't get away either. The thought should make you feel better.

✓ Out of frustration, don't be moody, bossy or irritated at anyone in your family.

✓ Don't pick a fight with your spouse to justify your affair or ease your conscience.

✓ Don't use a fight as an excuse to storm out of the house and run to your rendezvous. Your family doesn't have to suffer just because you want to meet your lover.

✓ Don't invent stupid reasons to leave home, even if it's for just for a few minutes, to meet up with your lover. You're bound to look hurried when you grab your bag, throw on your coat and run down out the door. Your sharp movements will tell your spouse you're not running to get gas for the car.

An affair can make you a little bit crazy. So, get it together before your family realizes what is happening or you'll lose more than your mind.

When the need to be with your lover is overpowering pour your energies into something constructive for your family like taking the kids out to a movie, baking a cake from scratch, or finally painting that cabinet. Keep busy. The feeling will pass.

True Story

When an acquaintance found himself leaving home for an unscheduled quickie with his new lover, he happily slapped on some aftershave, grabbed his keys, snatched his attaché case as if he were meeting a colleague for an emergency meeting, and quickly ran out the door – but not before seeing his children's disappointed faces. The haunting picture wrecked his rendezvous. His running out on his family ruined their evening.

Chapter 10

When It's Over

So Long, Babe!

One day your affair will be over.

If you want to end the affair, then you must play fair. Sit with your lover, explain that you cannot see them any longer due to your guilty conscience, your need to be with your family, or whatever other reason you have. Be as honest and as straight forward as you can. It will be far less painful if you're telling the truth.

You can only hope your lover will be as considerate should they decide to end the affair. If the affair is waning and you find your lover has become hesitant, or started giving nonsensical reasons, or no reasons at all for their illogical behavior, just let them go. Some people simply don't know how to end it and find it hard to articulate their reasons and many can't even look you in the eye when they have to express themselves.

They're obviously frightened by their inability to endure the pressures of an affair, or perhaps feel their spouse suspects something. Whatever the reason, again, just let them go. Be thankful for the good times you had together and for not having been caught.

After all the adjustments you made to ensure a safe and successful affair, you'll now have to make changes once again, after the end of one.

> ✓ Till now you've been creative, calculating and on your toes every minute of every day. You will feel a sudden lull; a let-up of pressure and it will change your mood. You may even feel a little lost, and even lonely, but give it some time. Your life will readjust and get back to normal.

✓ If you were never found out, congratulate yourself for getting it right! There's no reason to be hurt when it's over. Fill up your free time with your family. More than likely you'll find you actually missed them. Again, don't overcompensate for the time you were away. Just enjoy getting closer to them again. The affair was great, but home is where the heart is.

✓ Be prepared for a sense of loss no matter who ended the affair. It is imperative that you remember you aren't pining away for the person but for the adventure, the excitement, and the sexual tension and release that made you feel so vibrant before.

✓ Talk it out. A therapist can help you come to terms with the new situation, get rid of any anger, resentment, thoughts of revenge and tears. Take a long drive and talk to yourself. Don't keep it bottled up. Find a safe outlet to vent.

✓ Don't call, stalk, or revisit places where you used to meet.

✓ If you ended the affair, don't get sucked in to meeting up again if your ex-lover pleads to meet one more time. Remind yourself why you broke it off and stick with your decision. Meeting again can only send mixed messages. Explain that it's over, it's hard on you too, but you cannot meet. Don't buckle. If your lover broke it off, they wouldn't want you calling them either.

✓ Getting over long term affairs is always harder because you both committed to each other, remembered birthdays, helped each other through problems, and maybe even discussed being together in the future. There is nothing that can be said to make this any easier except that time and distance will eventual help. You'll find your life adjusting in time, and you'll be laughing when you thought you would never laugh again.

True Story

A close friend ended a long-term relationship. While it was the right thing to do, she was still resentful over his lies and insincerity toward the end. She did not have closure, but she refused to meet him ever again, even to settle the score. Instead, she took her dog to the park and talked to it when they sat on the grass. She would have a cup of coffee at home and share some of her cookies with the dog, all the while telling it her feelings and pouring out her rage. My friend talked to that dog until she felt she had come to terms with the situation, her decision to leave, and new life. The dog gained two pounds, but my friend is content.

✓ If you are angry that your lover ended the affair, go the gym. It will get rid of a lot of tension. Oddly enough, now you won't look good for them, but in spite of them! If they see you one day on the street and you look like a homeless person, you'll hate yourself. Work out, trim out, look hot. You know the saying 'the best revenge is looking good'. In any case, it will be the time to open a new look and chapter in your life.

Back to Reality!

✓ Don't worry if you still fantasize about your lover when you make love with your spouse. It will stop in time.

✓ When you kiss your spouse think about what turns you on about them. Return your sexual focus back to your partner.

✓ Throw out all sex toys, condoms, maps, or anything incriminating you may still have stashed away. Switch up your perfume or cologne again for a fresh start.

When you start going through the "Who Am I Now?" stage you'll find you're basically the same person you were before you began the affair. But now you should feel a new confidence and feel a little bit wiser. Not only did you successfully achieve something you really felt you needed to do, but you also did it without hurting yourself, your partner or your family. You made sure there was a home and family to come back to.

Conclusion

Now that you've read through this guide, imagine having an affair with your spouse. You were willing to risk everything to be with a stranger but now think of having an affair, packed with the same intrigue, passion, excitement, and commitment, with the person you married.

Buy the sexy underwear. Wear the special perfumes. Meet in strange, out of the way places. Have sex in new positions. Seduce each other like you did when you first met. Make your partner want to run home to you, to make love with you. Make your spouse your lover.

BUT, if you find you still want to pursue an affair, then re-read this book and remember the rules.

You're going to need them...
The Author